Michigan

by the Capstone Press
Geography Department

Capstone Books

an imprint of Capstone Press
Mankato, Minnesota

Capstone Books are published by Capstone Press
Good Counsel Drive, P.O. Box 669, Mankato, Minnesota 56002
http://www.capstone-press.com

Printed in the United States of America.

Library of Congress Cataloging-in-Publication Data

Michigan/by the Capstone Press Geography Department
p. cm.--(One Nation)
Includes bibliographical references and index.
Summary: Surveys the history, geography, and people of Michigan.
ISBN 1-56065-436-8
1. Michigan--Juvenile literature. [1. Michigan.]
I. Capstone Press. Geography Dept. II. Series.
F566.3.M53 1996
977.4--dc20

96-23439
CIP
AC

Photo credits
Root Resources, cover, 10, 18, 30, 32.
Michigan Travel Bureau, 4, 5, 8, 15, 17, 22, 26, 28, 34, 37.
FPG, 6.
Archive Photos, 21.
James Rowan, 25.

Table of Contents

Fast Facts about Michigan 4

Chapter 1 The Motown Sound 7

Chapter 2 The Land.................................... 11

Chapter 3 The People.................................. 17

Chapter 4 Michigan History.......................... 23

Chapter 5 Michigan Business 31

Chapter 6 Seeing the Sights 35

Michigan Time Line 40

Famous Michiganders 42

Glossary 44

To Learn More 46

Internet Sites 46

Useful Addresses 47

Index 48

Words in **boldface** type in the text are defined in the Glossary in the back of this book.

Fast Facts about Michigan

State Flag

Location: In the Great Lakes region of the Midwestern United States

Size: 56,809 square miles (147,703 square kilometers)

Population: 9,817,242 (1998 U.S. Census Bureau figures)

Capital: Lansing

Date admitted to the Union: January 26, 1837; the 26th state

Robin

Largest cities:
Detroit, Grand Rapids, Warren, Flint, Lansing, Sterling Heights, Ann Arbor, Livonia, Dearborn, Westland

Apple blossom

Nickname: The Wolverine State
State bird: Robin
State flower: Apple blossom
State tree: White pine
State song: "Michigan, My Michigan" by Douglas M. Malloch

White pine

Chapter 1

The Motown Sound

Diana Ross, Michael Jackson, and Stevie Wonder have something in common. They rose to fame recording songs for Motown Records.

The Motown Sound started in Detroit in 1959. Berry Gordy Jr. opened a recording studio. It was called Hitsville USA. Gordy and his team combined gospel, rhythm and blues, and rock. The music had a new sound.

The drums set the beat. Electric bass guitars joined the rhythm. Saxophones and strings played accents off the beat. The lead singers started the verse, and the backup singers crooned. These were the marks of the Motown Sound.

Motown is Detroit's nickname. Detroit is also called the Motor City because so many cars are made there.

Diana Ross was an early Motown Records star.

Hitsville USA

True to its name, Gordy's studio produced hit after hit. Smokey Robinson and the Miracles sang "Shop Around." Mary Wells did "My Guy." Diana Ross and the Supremes sang "Where Did Our Love Go."

Gordy moved Motown Records to California in 1971. He sold the company in 1984. Motown continues to produce hits. Boyz II Men recorded songs for Motown.

Today, Hitsville USA is the Motown Museum. Photographs of famous Motown groups line the walls. Visitors can see the gold and platinum records of Motown hits.

Other Michigan Hits

Michigan attracts people throughout the year. Michiganders and visitors enjoy its sandy beaches in the summer. Colorful leaves bring many people to Michigan each fall. Skiers travel to its northern slopes in the winter. Tulips and cherry blossoms brighten the landscape each spring.

Skiers travel to Michigan's northern slopes in the winter.

5297

Chapter 2

The Land

Michigan is in the Great Lakes region of the Midwest. Four of the five Great Lakes border the state. They are Lakes Superior, Michigan, Huron, and Erie.

The lakes create most of Michigan's 3,288 miles (5,260 kilometers) of shoreline. Only Alaska has a longer shoreline.

Michigan is the only state made up of two **peninsulas**. The Mackinac Straits separate the Upper Peninsula from the Lower Peninsula. Together, the two peninsulas cover 56,809 square miles (147,703 square kilometers) of land.

Four of the five Great Lakes border Michigan.

The Western Upper Peninsula

The Superior Upland covers the western Upper Peninsula. This is rugged, hilly land. Michigan's highest point is in the Superior Upland. Mount Arvon reaches 1,979 feet (603 meters) above sea level.

The western Upper Peninsula has rich natural resources. Trees in the Ottawa National Forest rise above the land. Deposits of iron **ore** and copper lie under the ground.

The Eastern Upper Peninsula

The Great Lakes Plains stretches across the eastern Upper Peninsula. The Hiawatha National Forest covers much of this land. Forests of valuable maple trees grow there.

About 150 waterfalls tumble in the woods. Upper Tahquamenon Falls is 50 feet (15 meters) high. It is more than 200 feet (60 meters) wide. This makes Tahquamenon the second largest falls east of the Mississippi River. Only Niagara Falls is bigger.

The Lower Peninsula

The Great Lakes Plains continues across the entire Lower Peninsula. Trees cover much of the northern Lower Peninsula. Michigan's largest inland lake lies there. This is Houghton Lake. It covers 31 square miles (81 square kilometers).

Land in the Lower Peninsula ranges from hilly to flat. Tall sand dunes run down to Lake Michigan in the west. Sleeping Bear Dune is 480 feet (144 meters) high. The Irish Hills rise in southeastern Michigan.

Michigan's lowest elevation is along Lake Erie. It is 572 feet (172 meters) above sea level.

The southern Lower Peninsula has Michigan's richest soil. Large crops of fruit and vegetables grow well there.

Climate

The Upper and Lower Peninsulas have different weather. The Upper Peninsula is colder year-round. More than 160 inches (406 centimeters) of snow fall there each winter. Summer days are warm, but summer nights are cool.

Summer months are warmer in the Lower Peninsula. They are also more humid. This part of Michigan receives less than 40 inches (102 centimeters) of snow.

Tahquamenon Falls is near Paradise in the Upper Peninsula.

Wildlife

Deer, black bear, badgers, beaver, and bobcats live in Michigan's forests. Moose live on Isle Royale. They share this Lake Superior island with timber wolves. Elk have been reintroduced in the northern Lower Peninsula.

Gulls and herons nest in Michigan Islands National Wildlife Refuge. Smelt, salmon, and trout swim in Michigan's lakes, rivers, and streams.

2

Chapter 3

The People

Only seven states have more people than Michigan. About 84 percent of Michiganders are white. Many of their **ancestors** settled in Michigan during the 1800s. They came from eastern states, Canada, and European countries.

Many early Michiganders worked in Michigan's mines and forests. Other settlers started farms or built cities.

Thousands more people moved to Michigan in the 1900s. They found jobs in automobile plants and other factories. Many of these new Michiganders were African Americans.

Michigan's residents enjoy many winter sports.

Bavarian-style architecture is found in Frankenmuth.

Michigan's population growth has slowed down in recent years. Many Michiganders left the state as auto companies laid off workers.

White Ethnic Groups

Many Michiganders have English, Irish, French, German, or Dutch backgrounds. Some trace their families back to Finland, Norway, or Sweden. Others have ancestors from Poland, Slovakia, Italy, Greece, or the Ukraine.

Some **ethnic groups** founded towns. Dutch settlers built Holland, Michigan, in 1847. Each May, Holland's Tulip Festival celebrates the city's Dutch heritage. Dancers perform wearing wooden shoes.

German missionaries from Bavaria settled Frankenmuth. Examples of Bavarian-style architecture can be seen in the town. Many Finnish communities are located in the Upper Peninsula.

Detroit has Greek, Italian, Irish, and German neighborhoods. A large number of Middle Eastern people also live in Detroit. Many of them are Lebanese, Palestinians, and Syrians. Each ethnic group has its own restaurants, grocery stores, and bakeries.

African Americans

About 13 percent of Michigan's residents are African American. Some of their ancestors came from the South after the Civil War (1861-1865). Many more African Americans came to Michigan after World War I (1914-1918). These African Americans wanted jobs in the state's factories.

Detroit has one of the nation's largest African-American communities. The Museum of African American History is in Detroit. Its exhibits show the achievements of African Americans.

Hispanic Americans

About 2 percent of Michiganders are Hispanic. Most of them are recent **immigrants** from Mexico. Other Spanish-speaking people have come from Colombia and El Salvador.

Many of Michigan's Hispanic people work in the state's industries. Others find seasonal jobs on Michigan farms and **orchards**.

Asian Americans

Less than 2 percent of Michiganders have Asian backgrounds. Many of them came from India, Taiwan, Korea, the Philippines, and Vietnam.

Native Americans

Fewer than 56,000 Native Americans live in Michigan. They are from the Chippewa, Ottawa, Potawatomi, and Cherokee tribes.

Detroit's Museum of African American History shows the achievements of blacks, including Dr. Martin Luther King.

Many of Michigan's Native Americans live on **reservations**. There are eight small reservations in the state.

Reservations at Watersmeet, Hanniville, and St. Ignace host powwows each year. Tribal members perform traditional dances. They wear feathered and beaded clothing.

Chapter 4

Michigan History

Michigan's first people arrived about 12,000 years ago. They mined copper on Isle Royale and on the Upper Peninsula.

About 1,500 Native Americans lived in Michigan by the 1600s. The Chippewa and Menominee lived on the Upper Peninsula. The Ottawa, Miami, Potawatomi, and Huron lived on the Lower Peninsula.

The French in Michigan

French explorers canoed from Canada to Michigan in the 1600s. They called Canada and the Great Lakes area New France.

Lansing became Michigan's capital in 1847, 10 years after Michigan became a state. Detroit was the first capital.

Father Jacques Marquette started a **mission** at Sault Sainte Marie in 1668. This was Michigan's first non-Indian settlement.

French traders got beaver **pelts** from the Native Americans. They shipped the furs to Europe. The French built forts in Michigan to protect the fur trade. Fort Pontchartrain later became the city of Detroit.

The English in Michigan

England had set up 13 colonies along the Atlantic Ocean. The English, like the French, traded in furs. England took control of New France in 1763.

Pontiac, an Ottawa chief, led Native Americans against the English. The English won the war against Pontiac.

The Road to Statehood

England's 13 colonies won their independence in 1783. The United States was born. Michigan became part of the new nation. However, it was not a state yet.

Father Jacques Marquette started a mission at Sault Sainte Marie in 1668.

American settlers started arriving in Michigan in 1825. Most of them came from eastern states. They traveled on the Erie Canal and Lake Erie to Detroit. They built farms in the western and southern Lower Peninsula.

Michigan had enough people to become a state in 1832. But a fight over land near Toledo, Ohio, had to be settled first. Ohio got Toledo, and

TEXACO
REG. T.M.
SERVICE
20

Michigan got the western Upper Peninsula. Michigan became the 26th state on January 26, 1837.

Industry in the Young State

Mining on the Upper Peninsula became the state's first big business. Copper and iron ore were shipped along the Great Lakes. The Soo Canal was finished in 1855. Ore **barges** then traveled between Lake Superior and Lake Huron.

The Civil War broke out in 1861. Michigan ore helped build weapons for the North. About 90,000 Michiganders fought for the North against the South. No fighting took place in Michigan. The North won the war in 1865.

Michigan's population grew fast after the war. More farmers moved into southern Michigan. Lumberjacks cut down trees in the northern forests. Michigan led the nation in lumber production by 1870.

The Auto Industry Begins

Michigan became an important center for making cars. Ransom Olds started the Olds Motor

The Henry Ford Museum in Dearborn features exhibits on Michigan's auto industry.

Tourism is important to Michigan's economy. The Upper Peninsula offers biking near Lake of the Clouds.

Works in Detroit in 1899. Henry Ford founded the Ford Motor Company in Dearborn in 1903.

Auto plants were also built in Lansing and Flint. Detroit became the Automobile Capital of the World. Its nickname was the Motor City.

The Great Depression and World War II

The Great Depression (1929-1939) hurt the United States economy. Millions of Americans lost their jobs. Few people had money to buy cars. Thousands of Michigan autoworkers lost their jobs.

World War II (1939-45) helped end the Great Depression. Michigan auto plants began to make military vehicles. They built tanks, trucks, jeeps, and airplanes. About 600,000 Michiganders served in the armed forces.

Recent Times

Race relations became a problem in the 1960s. Some African Americans in Detroit rioted in 1967. Poor housing and working conditions angered them.

Michigan's auto industry had big problems in the 1970s. Many people were buying smaller Japanese cars. Thousands of Michigan workers were laid off. Others had their wages cut. Detroit then started making smaller, energy-efficient cars.

The state's leaders looked for new industries. Tourism in northern Michigan has grown. The state's oil and gas deposits now help the economy. Many computer-related businesses have started in the state.

J. BURTON AYERS

Chapter 5
Michigan Business

Service industries make up the largest part of Michigan's economy. Shipping and tourism are major Michigan service businesses. Manufacturing is the second-biggest part of the economy. Agriculture, mining, and lumbering are also important.

Shipping and Tourism

Michigan lies at the heart of Great Lakes shipping. Freighters carry goods around the world from Michigan's 50 ports. Some of these ships travel through the Soo Canals. The canals connect Lakes Superior and Huron.

A freighter unloads gravel at Port Huron. Shipping is a major Michigan business.

Iron ore is mined near Ispheming on the Upper Peninsula.

Tourism brings about $9 billion to Michigan each year. Tourists use the state's hotels, resorts, ski slopes, and campsites.

Manufacturing

Michigan is the nation's leading manufacturer of automobiles. The state's workers also make trucks, buses, boats, and airplanes.

Many Michiganders process food. Battle Creek is the world's leading maker of breakfast cereal.

The country's largest maker of baby food is in Fremont.

Agriculture

Michigan has many dairy cows. They help make the state a leading milk producer. Beef cattle, chickens, turkeys, and hogs are other Michigan livestock.

The state's largest crops are corn, wheat, sugar beets, and potatoes. Michigan is a leading grower of apples, cherries, and grapes. No other state produces as many cucumbers for pickles. Christmas tree farms produce millions of trees each year.

Mining and Logging

Iron ore and copper mines are on the Upper Peninsula. Only Minnesota produces more iron ore than Michigan. Natural gas fields lie in the northern Lower Peninsula. The Lower Peninsula also has about 6,000 active oil wells.

Loggers harvest maple trees in the Upper Peninsula. A log of bird's-eye maple once sold for $3,000.

Chapter 6
Seeing the Sights

Michigan has a variety of activities and sights. Hiking, fishing, and skiing attract many tourists. Others like to visit Michigan's towns and cities.

The Upper Peninsula

Michigan's only national park is on Isle Royale. This island is northwest of the Upper Peninsula in Lake Superior. Tourists reach the island by boat or **seaplane**. Visitors on its trails might see a moose.

Mountains cover much of the western Upper Peninsula. Lake of the Clouds is high in the Porcupine Mountains. This clear, deep lake mirrors the sky.

The mountains are known for ski resorts. Their vertical drops are the steepest in the Midwest.

Motor traffic is not allowed on Mackinac Island.

Indian Mountain Resort is near Wakefield. Its vertical drop is 638 feet (191 meters).

The town of Ispheming is to the east. The National Ski Hall of Fame and Museum is there. It has copies of the oldest-known ski and ski pole.

Sault Sainte Marie is at the Upper Peninsula's northeastern tip. A two-hour boat tour takes passengers through the Soo **Locks**.

St. Ignace is in the southeastern Upper Peninsula. Father Jacques Marquette is buried there. The Museum of Ojibwa Culture is nearby. Visitors learn about Native Americans and French traders.

The northern end of the five-mile-long Mackinac Bridge is in St. Ignace. This bridge crosses the Straits of Mackinac. It links the Upper Peninsula to the Lower Peninsula.

The Northern Lower Peninsula

Mackinac Island lies in the Straits of Mackinac. Visitors reach the island by plane or ferryboat. They tour the island in carriages, on bicycles, or on foot. Motor traffic is not allowed.

Fort Michilimackinac is a restored French fort from 1715.

Fort Mackinac is a highlight of the island. The British built it in 1780. Many visitors stay at the Grand Hotel. It dates to 1887.

Mackinaw City is on the southern end of the Mackinac Bridge. Fort Michilimackinac is the restored French fort from 1715.

Visitors like to fish in the northern Lower Peninsula. Trout fishing is very good in the Au Sable River.

The Southern Lower Peninsula

Grand Rapids lies in the southeastern Lower Peninsula. Gerald Ford grew up in this city. He became the 38th president of the United States. The Gerald R. Ford Museum tells his life story.

Kalamazoo lies to the south. The Kalamazoo Air Zoo has a flight simulator and restored aircraft.

Battle Creek is to the east. It is home to the Kellogg and Post cereal plants. The Cereal Festival features the world's longest breakfast table each June.

Lansing is to the northeast. It is the state capital. College students crowd Ann Arbor to the southeast. The main campus of the University of Michigan is there.

Dearborn lies farther east. Visitors enjoy the Henry Ford Museum and Greenfield Village. The museum tells the story of machines in the United States. Greenfield Village includes nearly 100 historic buildings. Visitors can see Thomas Edison's laboratory and Henry Ford's birthplace.

Detroit

Detroit lies in southeastern Michigan on the Detroit River. This is Michigan's largest city. It is just north of Windsor, Canada.

The towers of the huge Renaissance Center rise along the city's riverfront. This center is so big that it has its own zip code. Detroit's tallest building is the center's hotel.

Detroit is still known as the Motor City. The Detroit Grand Prix is held there every June. It is an auto race run on Belle Isle in the Detroit River. The city hosts the International Auto Show each January.

Michigan Time Line

10,000 B.C.—The first people arrive in Michigan.

1620—First French explorers reach Michigan.

1701—Fort Pontchartrain is built on the site of present-day Detroit.

1763—England gains control of Michigan.

1783—The United States gains control of Michigan.

1837—Michigan becomes the 26th state.

1844—Iron ore is discovered in the Upper Peninsula at Negaunee.

1854—The Republican anti-slavery party is founded in Jackson.

1855—The Soo Canal is completed between Lake Huron and Lake Superior.

1896—Charles King of Detroit is the first person to test drive a gasoline-powered automobile in Michigan.

1899—The first auto factory opens in Detroit.

1908—General Motors Corporation is formed in Detroit

1935—The United Auto Workers union is formed to fight for better wages in Michigan's auto plants.

1942—The first B-24 bomber rolls off the assembly line at the Willow Run Bomber Plant near Ypsilanti.

1957—The Mackinac Bridge opens to traffic.

1967—Race riots cause 43 deaths in Detroit.

1977—The 73-story hotel in Detroit's Renaissance Center opens.

1988—Scientists discover a fungus that covers 37 acres (15 hectares) of forest near Crystal Falls.

1989 and 1990—The Detroit Pistons win the National Basketball Association (NBA) championship.

1993—The University of Michigan wins the Rose Bowl.

1997 and 1998—The Detroit Red Wings win the Stanley Cup hockey championship.

Famous Michiganders

Ralph Bunche (1904-1971) Statesman who helped found the United Nations; became the first African American to win the Nobel Peace Prize in 1950; born in Detroit.

Antoine de la Mothe Cadillac (1658-1730) French explorer who built Fort Ponchartrain, which later became the city of Detroit.

Madonna Louise Ciccone (1958-) Popular singing star and movie actress, better known simply as Madonna; born in Bay City.

George Armstrong Custer (1839-1876) Cavalry officer who was killed at the Battle of the Little Bighorn in Montana; spent his childhood in Michigan.

Edna Ferber (1887-1968) Novelist whose works such as *Show Boat*, *Saratoga Trunk*, and *Giant* were made into films; born in Kalamazoo.

Earvin "Magic" Johnson (1959-) Basketball star with the Los Angeles Lakers; named the NBA's most valuable player in 1987, 1989, and 1990; born in East Lansing.

W. K. Kellogg (1860-1951) Inventor of corn flakes and founder of the Kellogg Company; born in Battle Creek.

Charles Lindbergh (1902-1974) Became the first person to pilot a non-stop, solo airplane flight across the Atlantic Ocean in 1927; born in Detroit.

Joe Louis (1914-1981) Heavyweight boxing champion for 12 years; born in Alabama and grew up in Detroit.

Stevie Wonder (1950-) Musician and singer who became an international star with Motown Records; born in Saginaw.

Coleman Young (1918-) First African-American mayor of Detroit from 1973 to 1993; moved to Detroit when he was five years old.

Glossary

ancestor—a person from whom one is descended, such as a grandmother or a great-grandfather

barge—a long, flat boat used for hauling cargo

ethnic group—people with a common culture

immigrant—a person who comes to another country to settle

lock—a section of a canal closed off with gates in which a boat can be raised or lowered by pumping water in or out

mission—headquarters of people sent to do religious or charitable work in a territory or foreign country

orchard—area planted with fruit trees

ore—a mineral that contains valuable metal

pelt—animal skin

peninsula—land bordered by water on three sides

reservation—land set aside for Native Americans

seaplane—an airplane that can take off from and land in water

To Learn More

Brill, Marlene Targ. *Michigan.* Celebrate the States. New York: Benchmark Books, 1998.

Hintz, Martin and R. Conrad Stein. *Michigan.* New York: Children's Press, 1998.

Thompson, Kathleen. *Michigan.* Austin, Texas: Raintree Steck-Vaughn, 1996.

Wills, Charles A. *A Historical Album of Michigan.* Brookfield, Conn.: Millbrook Press, 1996.

Internet Sites

City.Net Michigan
http://www.city.net/countries/united_states/michigan
Magic Index of Michigan
http://www.govern.com.state.htm
Michigan Historical Center
http://www.sos.state.mi.us/history/history.html
Travel.org-Michigan
http://travel.org/michigan.html

Useful Addresses

Henry Ford Museum and Greenfield Village
20900 Oakwood Boulevard
Dearborn, MI 48124

Iron Mountain Iron Mine
U.S. Highway 2
Vulcan, MI 49801

Motown Historical Museum
2648 West Grand Boulevard
Detroit, MI 48208

Soo Locks Boat Tours
515 East Portage Avenue
Sault Sainte Marie, MI 49783

Wooden Shoe Factory
447 U.S. Highway 31
Holland, MI 49422

Index

Battle Creek, 32, 38

cereal, 32, 38
Civil War, 19, 27

Edison, Thomas, 38

Ford, Gerald R., 38
Ford, Henry, 38

Great Depression, 28-29
Great Lakes, 11, 23, 27, 31
Great Lakes Plains, 13

Houghton Lake, 13

Isle Royale, 35

Lansing, 5, 28, 38

Marquette, Jacques, 24, 36
Motor City, 7, 28, 39
Motown, 7, 9
Mount Arvon, 12

Pontiac, 24

reservations, 21

settlers, 17, 25
Soo Canal, 27, 31
Superior Upland, 12

Tahquamenon Falls, 13

World War I, 19
World War II, 28-29